W9-DHH-544

HOW TO Draw Graphic Novels!

by
VICTOR M. DAVILA

tangerine Press®

an imprint of

SCHOLASTIC

www.scholastic.com

Dedicated to my wife, Me-Linh and my parents, Victor & Carmen, who have all lovingly supported my obsession with art and comics.

All rights reserved. No part of this publication may be reproduced, or stored in a retrieval system, or transmitted in any form or by any means, electronic, mechanical, photocopying, recording, or otherwise, without written permission from Tangerine Press.

Copyright ©2004 Scholastic Inc.

Scholastic and Tangerine Press and associated logos are trademarks of Scholastic, Inc.

Published by Tangerine Press, an imprint of Scholastic Inc, 557 Broadway, New York, NY 10012

10 9 8 7 6 5 4 3 2 1

ISBN: 0-439-66469-1

Printed and bound in China.

DISTRIBUTED IN CANADA BY:
SCHOLASTIC CANADA, LTD.
175 HILLMOUNT ROAD
MARKHAM, ONTARIO
L6C 1Z7

DISTRIBUTED IN AUSTRALIA BY:
SCHOLASTIC AUSTRALIA
REPLY 110
PO BOX 525
GOSFORD NSW 2250

Table of Contents!

So You Wanna Draw?

"GRAPHIC NOVELS" IS ANOTHER NAME FOR COMIC BOOKS. WHILE REGULAR NOVELS ARE MADE UP OF ONLY WORDS, GRAPHIC NOVELS ARE MADE UP OF WORDS AND GRAPHICS, OR DRAWINGS WHICH IS WHERE *YOU* COME IN!

ILLUSTRATORS HAVE MANY *DIFFERENT STYLES*. BUT THERE'S ONE THING ALL ILLUSTRATORS HAVE IN COMMON: THEY WERE ALL KIDS WHO DREAMED ONE DAY OF DRAWING THEIR FAVORITE SUPERHEROES! BEFORE YOU SIT DOWN TO DRAW GRAPHIC NOVELS, HOWEVER, YOU HAVE TO LEARN THE BASICS. THESE ARE RULES, GUIDELINES, TIPS, AND SUGGESTIONS THAT EVERY BUDDING ARTIST SHOULD KNOW BEFORE SETTING OFF ON A CAREER IN THE ILLUSTRATION FIELD.

AND REMEMBER, WHILE THESE GUIDELINES ARE IMPORTANT, THEY'RE NOT WRITTEN IN STONE. RULES ARE MEANT TO BE BENT, BROKEN, OR EVEN EXAGGERATED! MANY ARTISTS HAVE MADE GREAT AND MEMORABLE GRAPHIC NOVELS BY DOING THEIR OWN THING. SO JUST HAVE FUN AND LET YOUR *CREATIVITY FLOW!*

Tools of the Trade!

Every hero needs a utility belt! Below is what every artist needs to put in theirs! These supplies can be found in your local art or office supply store. You get an HB drawing pencil and 6 mini markers to start your adventures.

- Pencils (a variety of hards and softs. Try these: HB, 3H, 4B)
- White Vinyl Eraser
- Fine-tip Permanent Artist-quality Ink Pens (try sizes 01, 05, and 08!)
- French Curve
- Ames Lettering Guide
- Ruler
- Triangles (of different angles)
- T-square
- Black India Ink
- Process White (for ink corrections)
- Brushes of various sizes
- Crow Quill Dip Pens
- Brush Pen
- Tracing Paper
- Bristol Board
- Sketchbook

The Assembly Line!

Comic books and graphic novels are created by five people (not counting, of course, the editors and publishers – all **incredibly** important, too!): the writer, the penciler, the inker, the colorist, and the letterer. Sometimes, one person can handle more than one of these jobs, but these are the main **creative** responsibilities.

The job of the **Writer** is, obviously, to create the plot and dialogue of the comic book.

Once the writer turns in the script, the **Penciler** takes over. It's his or her job to interpret the writer's words into exciting panels of art that tell the story and keep the reader's attention.

Then the art goes to the **Inker**. It's the inker's job to strengthen the penciler's line drawings with ink.

Rounding off this team of graphic novel creatives are the **Colorist** and the **Letterer**. The colorist adds colors to the inked art and the letterer writes in the text, dialogue, and sound effects of the story.

Getting In Shape!

Shapes are the most basic elements of every drawing. Whatever you're drawing can be broken down into the simplest shapes. Look at your pencil– it's essentially a cylinder. Doesn't the pencil tip look a bit like a cone? And doesn't your television look kind of like a cube?

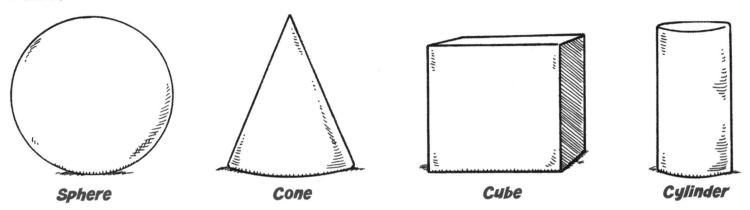

Sphere   *Cone*   *Cube*   *Cylinder*

By starting with these basic shapes, you can build all sorts of different items! Here are some things you probably see everyday that are made up of these basic shapes. Look around your house – can you spot other basic shapes?

You've Got Style!

Have you ever noticed that your favorite hero looks different depending on who draws him? That's because each artist comes from different artistic backgrounds with different artistic influences, and therefore injects his own style into the drawings. Below are examples of two popular drawing "styles."

I FEEL LIKE I'M LOOKING AT A *FUNHOUSE MIRROR!*

KEEP IT UP AND I'LL *SQUASH YOU LIKE A BUG!*

THE TRADITIONAL "COMIC BOOK" HERO HAS SLIGHTLY EXAGGERATED REALISTIC ANATOMY WITH CROSSHATCHED DETAILS.

THIS STYLE IS POPULARIZED BY CARTOONS. THE FIGURE'S PROPORTIONS ARE EXAGGERATED BUT SLEEK, AND THE OVERALL DESIGN IS KEPT SIMPLE.

It will take many years of illustrating before you develop your own style. In the meantime, study artists that inspire you, not only in graphic novels, but in all art forms.

Pattern Buffer!

Remember, a penciler should only pencil what the inker can ink. If you try shading with the side of your pencil lead, the inker won't be able to match that with ink and a thin-point inking tool. So that's why shadows and values are built with different line patterns.

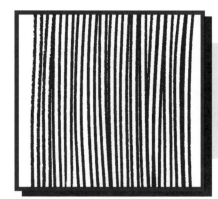

Parallel straight lines create an even shade. The closer the lines, the darker the shadow appears.

Diagonal instersecting sets of parallel lines create a darker shadow. This is called *Crosshatching.*

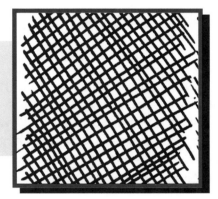

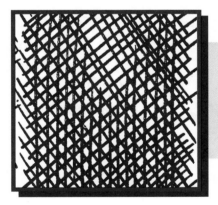

Introducing a third or more set of parallel lines to the crosshatching builds darker areas.

Stippling is a technique consisting of dot patterns created by hitting the pen repetitively on the paper. The closer the dots, the darker the area.

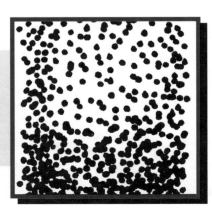

Into The Shadows!

The presence of a light source is what gives a shape it's form and dimension. Without the introduction of light and shadow, a drawing looks flat.

For example, Figure 1 below is nothing more than a flat circle. It has no dimension and no form. But as soon as a light source is added (Figure 2), shadows wrap around the circle giving it form. The circle now has dimension making it a sphere!

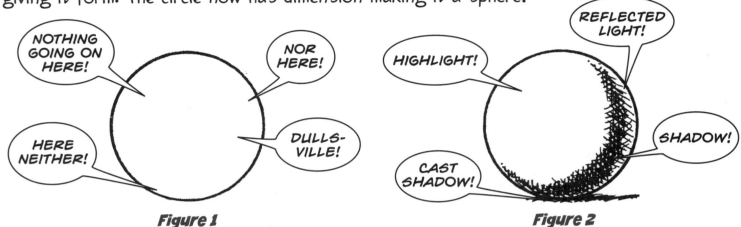

Figure 1   Figure 2

The same thing happens when you add shadow to a figure. But before you can begin drawing shadows, you have to figure out the postition of the light. The location of the light source will determine what is light, what is dark, and what falls somewhere in between. The area of an object that is the brightest is called the **Highlight**. The dark area is the **Shadow**. The shadow created by the object is called a **Cast Shadow**. The lighter area created by light bouncing of objects near the circle is the **Reflected Light.**

Into The Shadows!

Light and shadow are also vital in creating a mood or drama of a character or scene!

IN THIS DRAWING, THE LIGHT SEEMS TO BE HITTING THE FACE ON ALL SIDES, AND DOESN'T CONVEY ANY MOOD OR DRAMA.

INTRODUCING HARSH LIGHTING FROM OVERHEAD ENHANCES THE DRAMA AND GIVES A FEELING OF TENSION OR IMPENDING DOOM.

LIGHTING FROM UNDERNEATH CAUSES THE CHARACTER TO LOOK CREEPY OR EVIL.

Practice drawing shadows on the blank faces below. Try placing light sources in different positions to practice drawing different shadows on the face. Make a copy of these drawings before you draw on them in case you have to start over.

Figure It Out!

The ideal male *superhero* figure roughly stands 8½ heads tall. That means that if you drew the same head 8½ times on top of each other, that's how tall the hero would be.

Like the male, the female hero is also 8½ heads tall. However, the female head is slightly smaller than her male counterpart. The female has softer edges, to give her a more feminine look. Also, her waist is higher and her legs are longer than the male's, to give her a long, slender look.

Figure It Out!

Some of the typical superhero attributes include broad shoulders, a square chin, piercing eyes, and a winning smile! But don't feel as if you have to limit your characters to these rules. One of the fun things about designing characters is that you can let your imagination run wild! If you feel that the protector of your metropolitan city should be a stocky, 5-foot tall alien with frizzy hair, go for it! It's your character to design as you please!

Use the space next to the characters to draw your own character!

Head Games!

Like the body, the male and female heads have the same proportions. The male head is more angular than the female. The female has softer edges, to give her a more feminine look.

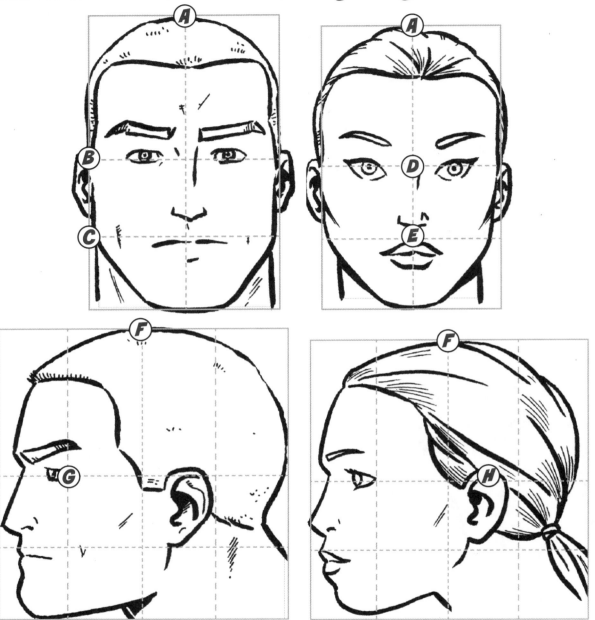

A. The head is about six eyes wide.

B. The head is divided in half at the *eyeline.*

C. Find the point halfway between the eyeline and the chin. That's the *noseline* (Actually, the nose is drawn a tad above that line).

D. Between the eyes is the width of an eye.

E. The mouth sits about ⅓ down between the noseline and the chin.

F. The head in profile roughly fits into a square and can be divided in four vertical equal parts.

G. The eye sits roughly at the intersection of the eyeline, and the first and second quadrants.

H. The ear sits between the eyeline and the noseline in the third quadrant. The top of the ear portrudes over the eyeline.

Head Games!

Once you understand the main elements of the head, rotate the angles to get different head positions.

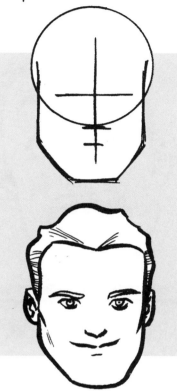 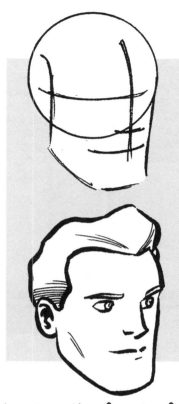 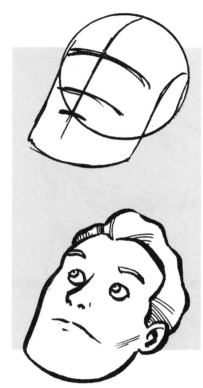

The same guidelines used when drawing the front of the face — the eyeline, the noseline, the mouth — are also used when drawing other views. Just remember to curve the lines to compensate for the roundness of the head.

Use this area to draw your hero's head in different positions!

You can tell what people are feeling by looking at the face. The shape of the mouth and eyes, and the direction of the eyebrows are all indicators of a person's emotional state. Study the samples below to see what features convey different emotions.

I'M REALLY *HAPPY!* LOOK HOW THE CORNERS OF MY MOUTH LIFT AND MY LOWER EYELIDS COME UP!

WOW! I'M *SURPRISED!* LOOK HOW MY EYES WIDEN AND MY EYEBROWS ARE RAISED! AND MY MOUTH IS WIDE OPEN!

UH, I'M *CONFUSED.* SEE HOW MY FEATURES AREN'T SYMMETRICAL? ONE EYEBROW IS UP, THE OTHER DOWN; ONE EYE IS WIDE, THE OTHER SMALL. AND MY MOUTH IS OPEN, BUT SMALL.

I'M SO *WORRIED!* LOOK AT THE CORNERS OF MY MOUTH POINT DOWNWARD, AND THE EYEBROWS SLANT UPWARDS! ALSO, MY EYES ARE A WIDE.

I'M VERY *SAD!* LOOK AT HOW MY EYES SQUINT, MY EYEBROWS SLANT UPWARD AND MY MOUTH IS CLOSED!

I'M SO *ANGRY!!* SEE MY EYEBROWS SLANT DOWNWARD, MY EYES SHRINK, MY NOSTRILS FLARE, AND MY TEETH CLENCH!

Face Facts!

Use this area to draw different facial expressions!

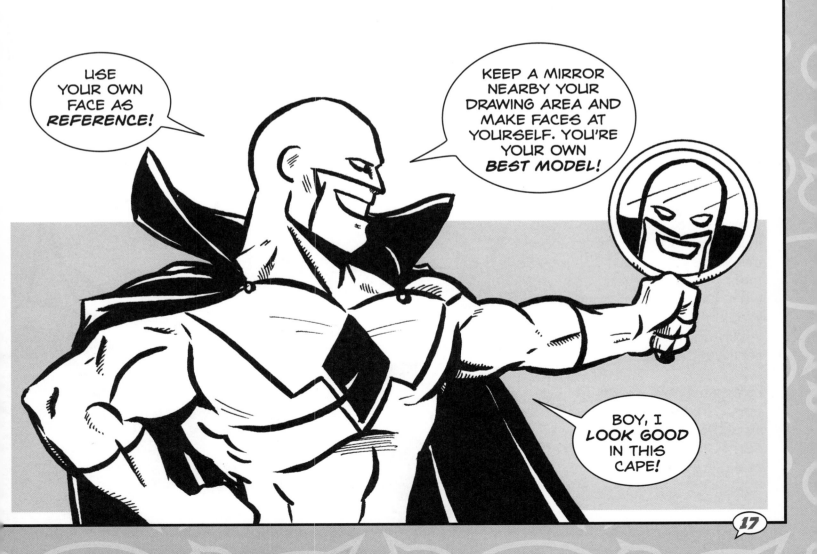

USE YOUR OWN FACE AS *REFERENCE!*

KEEP A MIRROR NEARBY YOUR DRAWING AREA AND MAKE FACES AT YOURSELF. YOU'RE YOUR OWN *BEST MODEL!*

BOY, I *LOOK GOOD* IN THIS CAPE!

What An Exaggeration!

You can create a variety of characters by exaggerating body shapes and features. Look at these examples of how simple changes in the face create different personalities:

MY HEAD HAS *NORMAL PROPORTIONS!*

SHRINKING AND MOVING THE FEATURES UP GIVES THE APPEARANCE OF A LARGE CHIN, SUGGESTING *STRENGTH!*

SHRINKING AND LOWERING THE FEATURES GIVES THE APPEARANCE OF A LARGE FOREHEAD, SUGGESTING *INTELLIGENCE!*

BIG EYES MAKE THE CHARACTER LOOK *YOUNG* OR *CUTE!*

Play around with your characters' proportions. Enlarge, shrink, or expand their features or body parts to come up with fun, humorous, strange, or even **scary** new characters! Doing so can also help inject personality into your character. A 9-foot tall muscle man looks even stronger with larger than normal arms. Wouldn't a creepy, clown-like villain look even scarier with a really wide, toothy smile?

Exaggeration plays a big part in graphic novels. And these characters just don't look cool, they're really fun to draw!

WHAT ARE *YOU LOOKING AT?!*

Blockheads!

Use shapes as inspirations to create new and unique looking characters! There's no telling what kind of cool heads you'll create. Below are three character heads based on basic shapes. Use the space on the right to create your own character heads based on these shapes!

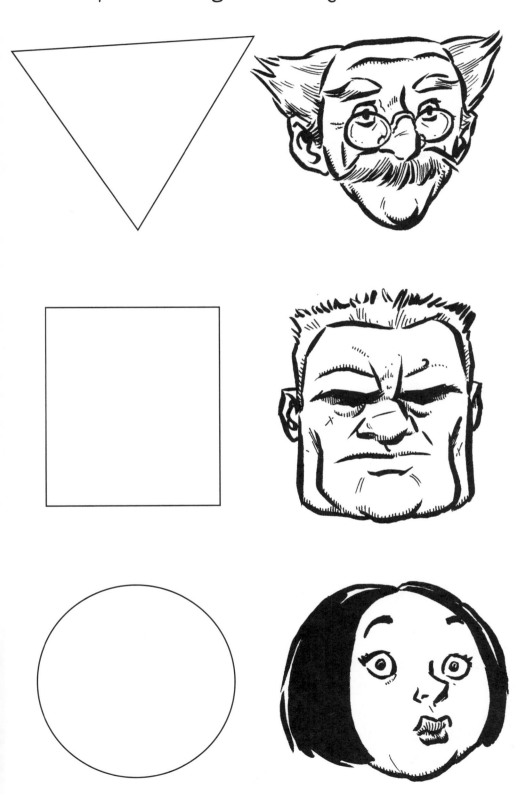

Shape Up!

The same thing applies to body shapes. Remember, not everybody in the world of graphic novels is a 6-foot tall muscle man. You can use all the shapes and principles you've learned so far to create really cool characters. Use the space on the right to create different characters based on the shapes on the left.

Shape Up!

So, how do regular guys stack up to superheros? Well, while the heroes are 8½ heads high, an "Average Joe" is roughly 6 to 6½ heads tall.

While the "Average Joe" above is muscular, you'll notice that he isn't as big as the superhero. Joe's shoulders are less broad, and his arms are slightly smaller. And while Joe may look like he's standing up straight, he doesn't stand as tall as the hero, who's always ready to jump into action!

The Clothes Make The Man!

Superhero costumes are supposed to be skin tight to show off their muscles. But regular clothes usually have excess fabric that accumulate near joints, such as elbows and knees. When the body turns or bends, the clothes react to those bends with folds. Keeping this in mind will help you draw the clothes more realistic and natural.

FOR EXAMPLE, HERE IS A MUSCULAR BENT ARM.

HERE, THE ARM IS CLOTHED, BUT THE SLEEVE IS OVERLY-TIGHT AND DOESN'T REACT TO THE BENT ARM. NOT VERY REALISTIC, IS IT?

HERE, THE BENT ARM IS CREATING NATURAL FOLDS, GIVING THE SLEEVE A MORE NATURAL LOOK.

MY ARCH ENEMY MUST'VE TAMPERED WITH MY *WASHING MACHINE* AGAIN!!

Button Poppin' Action!

Fold lines aren't used to show just bends and turns. Sometimes they're helpful in showing overly stretched areas in clothing.

For instance, in this drawing, notice how slight folds give a hint that the buttons are about to pop. While the bent areas show the bunching of fabric, the stretched areas don't have any folds. They're smooth and only show folds near the areas that are keeping them tight.

It's a good idea to look at men's and women's fashion magazines to get an idea of different hairstyles and fashion trends. They also have good examples of how clothing looks on a posed figure. They're a great source of photo reference!

It's also important to be familiar with different types of clothing – from the latest fashions, to everyday uniforms, to fantastical costumes!

Use the space below to practice drawing clothes on your characters!

All On The Surface!

Texture is the surface characteristic of an object. It's what identifies what the object is and how it feels. For example, the four spheres below are similar in size and shape. What distinguishes them from each other is the surface texture. The first two are smooth, the last two are rough and hairy. Without the textures, they'd just be regular circles.

Glass

Smooth

Rocky

Furry

The glass and smooth (i.e. metallic, rubber, etc.) spheres are similar except for the fact that the glass is transparent. Notice how they are both drawn with a smooth, unbroken outline, while the rough sphere has a wavy outline, and the furry sphere's outline is erratic.

The combination of different surface textures adds to the realism of your drawings — even if the subject is *fantastical*.

Take our rather fashionable alien friend here. The combination of the fur-lined cape, the metal head piece and wrist bands, and the rough skin help to strengthen the believability of the character.

Notice how in the case of the fur, the repetition of small broken lines of different sizes and thicknesses build the appearance of fur. And the number of small lines increases in the shadowy areas.

Less detail is needed on his face and arms, where only small dots and circles represent the scaly, rough skin.

I'VE TRIED SKIN LOTION, BUT *NOTHING* WORKS!

All On The Surface!

Nature is full of interesting textures — the rippling of water, the wind-blown sand of a desert, the scaly skin of a reptile. There are hundreds of types of wood, all with distinctive knots and waves.

As an artist, you need to be aware of such texture variety and how to make your line art represent those textures.

Use the line drawings below to practice illustrating different kinds of textures on everyday objects.

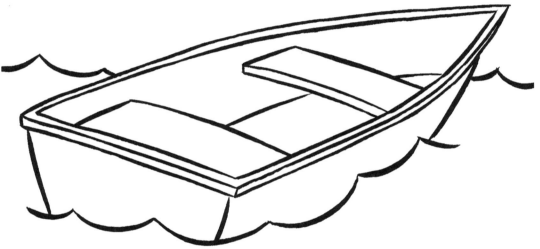

Give this wooden boat and choppy water texture!

Is this mug metal or glass?

smooth

What kind of rock is this— smooth or rough?

Strike A Pose!

What would graphic novels be without the characters in interesting and dynamic poses?!

To the left we have a hero running. The drawing's okay, but it's a pretty boring pose. Actually, he looks more like he's jogging than running! It lacks a sense of excitement and urgency.

Now this is more like it! This figure looks like he's really running fast! Wherever he's going, he needs to get there right away!

The dynamic of the pose is determined by the **Line of Action!** The line of action is an imaginary line that runs through the figure and determines the body's curve.

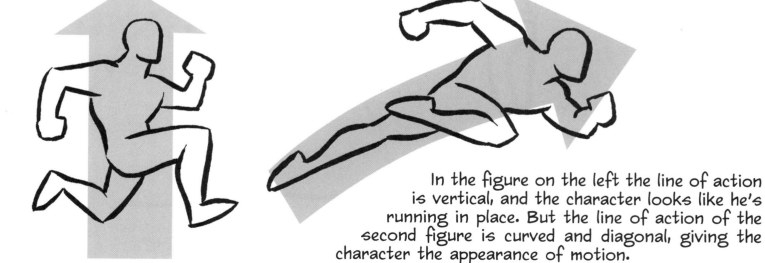

In the figure on the left the line of action is vertical, and the character looks like he's running in place. But the line of action of the second figure is curved and diagonal, giving the character the appearance of motion.

Strike A Pose!

Having a line of action that's mostly vertical, or up and down, will usually produce a stagnant figure. A diagonal line of action allows the figure to appear dynamic.

Use the space below to practice drawing action poses!

Don't Lose Perspective!

Many artists are intimidated at the thought of drawing backgrounds, mostly because they know they'll have to tackle **Perspective!** Perspective is how you show depth and distance or the third dimension. Have you ever looked down a long road and noticed that the road gets thinner and thinner until it ends at a point? That's perspective!

The point where the lines seem to meet is called the **Vanishing Point.** The horizontal line where the vanishing point sits is the **Horizon Line.** The horizon line represents the viewer's eye level.

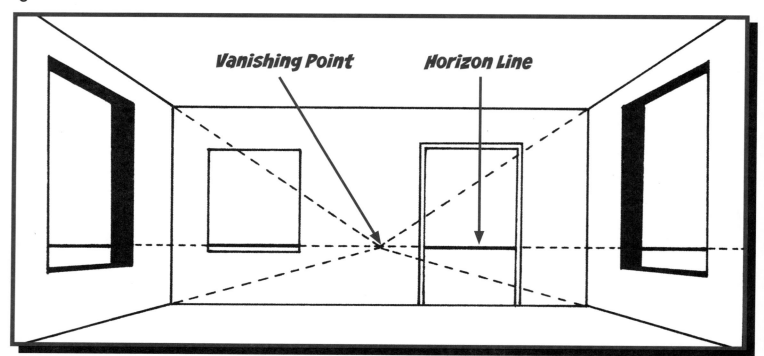

One-Point Perspective!

One-Point Perspective means the perspective only has one vanishing point. Notice that while the receding lines go into the vanishing point, the vertical and horizontal lines do not move away. They remain vertical or horizontal. Only the side lines that travel into the distance meet at the vanishing point.

Use the space below to practice drawing one-point perspective!

Don't Lose Perspective!

Two-Point Perspective!

Two-Point Perspective means the perspective has two vanishing points. Again notice that the vertical lines stay vertical, and don't recede to the vanishing point.

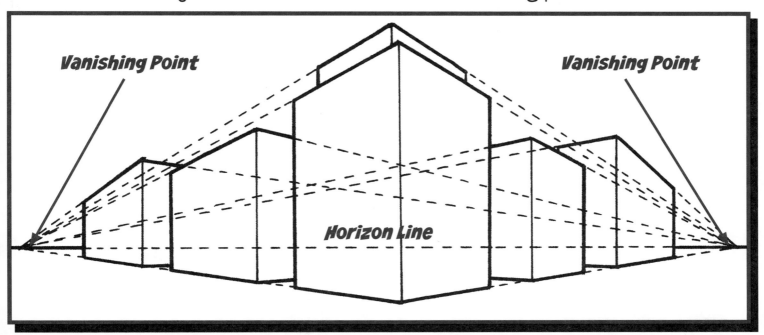

Use the space below to practice drawing two-point perspective!

Fly Off The Page!

One of the most common images seen in graphic novels is the superhero flying off the page towards you (just like the cover of this book!). This is done with a technique called **Foreshortening.** Foreshortening is when the figure is drawn in perspective. Using foreshortening can allow you to create exciting and heroic images.

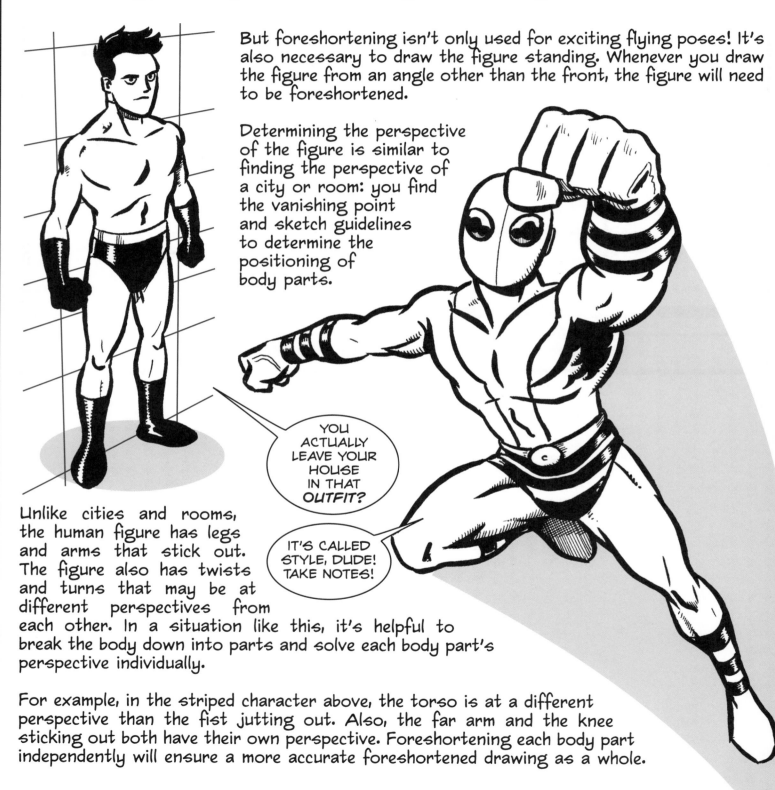

But foreshortening isn't only used for exciting flying poses! It's also necessary to draw the figure standing. Whenever you draw the figure from an angle other than the front, the figure will need to be foreshortened.

Determining the perspective of the figure is similar to finding the perspective of a city or room: you find the vanishing point and sketch guidelines to determine the positioning of body parts.

YOU ACTUALLY LEAVE YOUR HOUSE IN THAT *OUTFIT?*

IT'S CALLED STYLE, DUDE! TAKE NOTES!

Unlike cities and rooms, the human figure has legs and arms that stick out. The figure also has twists and turns that may be at different perspectives from each other. In a situation like this, it's helpful to break the body down into parts and solve each body part's perspective individually.

For example, in the striped character above, the torso is at a different perspective than the fist jutting out. Also, the far arm and the knee sticking out both have their own perspective. Foreshortening each body part independently will ensure a more accurate foreshortened drawing as a whole.

Fly Off The Page!

Sometimes you'll need to exaggerate the figure to make it look dynamic. However, there's no easy formula to make it easier. In situations like this, an artist will have to tweak something until it looks right.

THIS DRAWING SHOWS THE FORESHORTENED FIGURE WITH REALISTIC PROPORTIONS. NOTE THE FISTS ARE SMALLER THAN THE HEAD.

MAKING THE FISTS BIGGER GIVE THE DRAWING MORE *POWER.* NOW HE LOOKS LIKE HE'S FLYING RIGHT AT YOU.

Use the space below to practice foreshortening. Draw your hero flying off the page or swinging down with his legs coming right at you!

What's Your P.O.V.?

In order to add interest to the panels of the page, artists like to incorporate different shots and *Point of Views* (P.O.V.). Below are the most common "shots" artists use.

Wide Shot / Establishing Shot
The wide or establishing shot sets the location of where the action is taking place. Many times it's the first panel of a scene.

Long Shot
A long shot usually shows the full character from head to toe. It's good for dialogue between characters or to show a character in its surroundings.

Medium Shot
A medium shot is similar to a "long shot," but shows the characters from the waist up. It's also good for intimate character dialogue.

Closeup
A closeup is a tight shot of a character's face or an object. If it's a person, it's devised to show emotion. If it's an object, then it highlights the importance of that object.

Bird's Eye View
The bird's eye view is a view from above the action. It gives the reader a detached feeling and lets them see the action from an unusual perspective.

Worm's Eye View
The worm's eye view is a view from under the action. It lets the reader feel they're in the middle of the action.

Extreme Closeup
An extreme closeup is like a regular closeup, but even tighter on the person or object (the person's eyes, an inscription on a ring, etc.). It also shows emotion or importance.

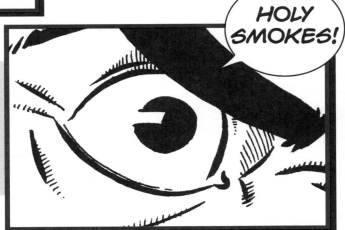

Thumbs Up To The Script!

Now it's time to translate the script into the words and pictures. Begin by reading, and then re-reading the script. Make notes as you go along. Better yet, doodle layout ideas in the script's margins. Many times, those initial concepts are what end up in the story's final layout!

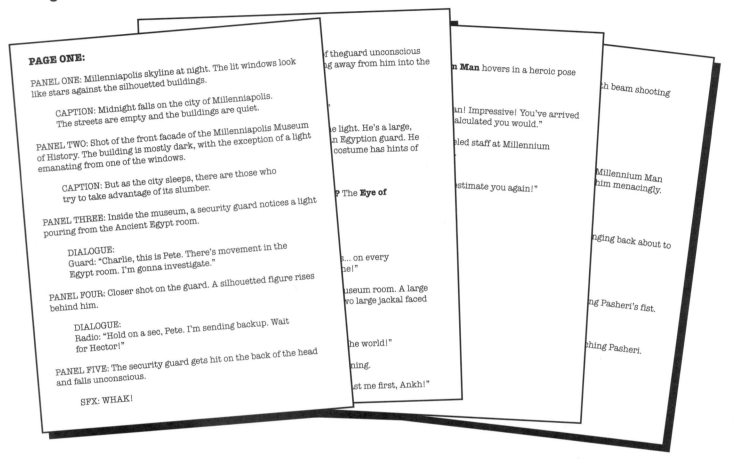

PAGE ONE:

PANEL ONE: Millenniapolis skyline at night. The lit windows look like stars against the silhouetted buildings.

> CAPTION: Midnight falls on the city of Millenniapolis. The streets are empty and the buildings are quiet.

PANEL TWO: Shot of the front facade of the Millenniapolis Museum of History. The building is mostly dark, with the exception of a light emanating from one of the windows.

> CAPTION: But as the city sleeps, there are those who try to take advantage of its slumber.

PANEL THREE: Inside the museum, a security guard notices a light pouring from the Ancient Egypt room.

> DIALOGUE:
> Guard: "Charlie, this is Pete. There's movement in the Egypt room. I'm gonna investigate."

PANEL FOUR: Closer shot on the guard. A silhouetted figure rises behind him.

> DIALOGUE:
> Radio: "Hold on a sec, Pete. I'm sending backup. Wait for Hector!"

PANEL FIVE: The security guard gets hit on the back of the head and falls unconscious.

> SFX: WHAK!

The next step is to start drawing a bunch of **Thumbnail Sketches.** Thumbnail sketches are very small sketches used to rough out the layout of your drawing. Think of it as creating a game plan of how you're going to draw your page!

Break down the page in your thumbnails and figure out the placement of the panels and how the story flows.

Thumbs Up To The Script!

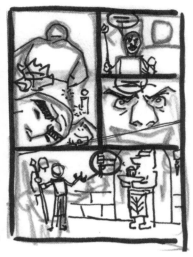

Include the placement of word balloons in your thumbnails. It's a good idea to start planning for them now. If you get too far into the layout design without considering the text, you may run out of room for them in your panels.

Keep drawing thumbnails until you're happy with a layout design. Keep in mind that thumbnails aren't supposed to be neat or even coherent to anyone else but you. Their sole purpose is to help the artist plan the page, so don't go into too much detail!

Time To Grow Up!

The pages of a graphic novel are usually drawn at the larger size of 10 x 15 (25cm x 38cm)*. This is the same aspect ratio as a 4 x 6 (10cm x 15cm) index card. After drawing your thumbnails, draw a tighter version of the layout on an unruled 4 x 6 (10cm x 15cm) index card. Then, enlarge the index card on a copier or a computer at 250 percent. Place the copy or printout on a lightboard, put a blank sheet of drawing paper over it, and trace your layout! That way you can keep the dynamics of your small drawing in your final page.

You can find unruled 4 x 6 (10cm x 15cm) index cards at your local office supply store.

4x6
(10cm X 15cm)
Index Card

250%

10 x 15 (10cm X 15cm) Drawing Paper

*This book, however, is 9 x 11 (22cm x 28cm), a different ratio than a typical graphic novel.

Laying It On The Line!

Remember, the most important thing to keep in mind when penciling a graphic novel is **clear storytelling!** This is especially important when you're laying out the story. Below are some samples of common page layouts.

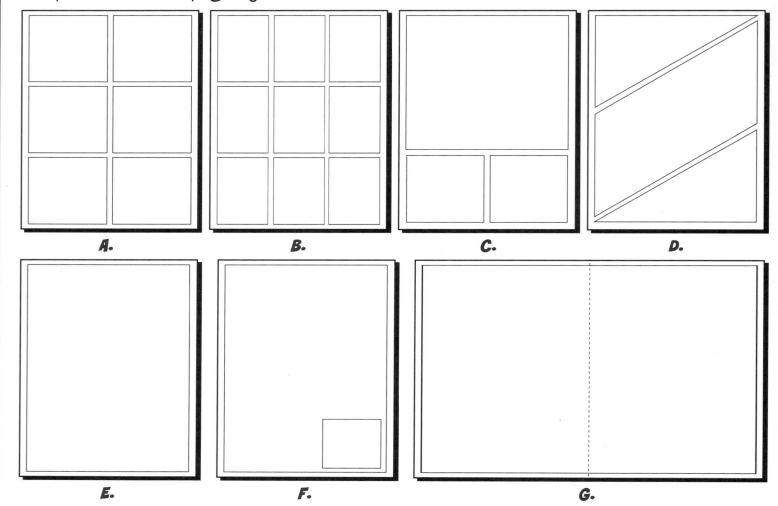

A.   B.   C.   D.

E.   F.   G.

A.-C. Standard Grid Page: The standard grid page is what most graphic novel pages are based on and has many varieties. These are just a few examples of how you can break down a page, but there are many more panel configurations you can create.

D. Diagonal Panels: Diagonal panels are often used to exhibit strange angles or to enhance the movement of a character.

E.-F. Splash Page: The splash page is another standard in the graphic novel pages. It's usually a full page panel (sometimes there's a smaller panel within the larger one). The splash page is usually reserved for important or climactic moments in the story. Sometimes you can combine the splash page with a smaller panel.

G. The Double Page Spread: The double page spread is a splash that takes up two pages. This is usually reserved for the **really** important or action packed moments of a story! The art on the spread may be drawn horizontal or vertical (which means the reader would have to turn the book sideways).

Keeping The Pace!

In a graphic novel, each panel represents a specific moment. If we compare it to time, this means that each panel captures less than one second of the action. Therefore, the more panels included in the moment, the slower the action; the fewer panels, the quicker the action. This is called *Pacing*.

For instance, this ball falls, hits the ground, and bounces off-panel in just three frames. The sequence only shows you the three most important moments that allow you to know exactly what happened to the ball.

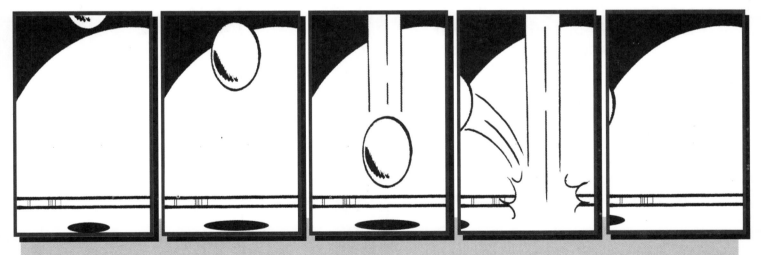

Here's the same ball going through the same action, but now it's taking five frames. The time it takes for this ball to bounce is almost double what it was in the first example. This is because the additional frames are capturing new moments and we perceive it as longer time.

Manipulating the pacing of the story can enhance its mood and emotion. Action sequences that are fast paced can benefit from quick cuts between panels. Suspenseful moments in stories can be more effective by using cleverly placed panels between the other panels of action.

Start Your Pencils!

Now that you've decided on the page layout, it's time to work on the final pencils. But which pencils should you use? Artists are choosy when it comes to art tools. Once they find something they like, they tend to stick with it! Below are some examples of available pencil varieties.

A. Graphite Pencil: The graphite pencil is the most common pencil. In fact, you have one that came with your kit! But did you know that it comes in **20 different varieties** of hard and soft? The varieties of pencils (from hardest to softest) are 9H, 8H, 7H, 6H, 5H, 4H, 3H, 2H, H, F, HB, B, 2B, 3B, 4B, 5B, 6B, 7B, 8B, and 9B. The harder the pencil the lighter the mark it will make. The softer the pencil, the darker the mark. The common #2 pencil is HB. This is the pencil in your kit. Try 3H, HB, and 4B for a good sampling of the different pencil types. Just make sure to keep a pencil sharpener handy! The softer leads tend to wear down fast!

B. Non-Photo Pencil: These non-reproductive pencils usually come in light blue. Many times, any blue pencil will do the job, as long as you draw lightly. Since the pencil marks don't reproduce when photocopied, the pencil marks don't have to be erased for printing.

C. Mechanical Pencil: The mechanical pencil is probably the handiest pencil to have. Lead is just a click away! They typically come in 0.5mm, 0.7mm, and 0.9mm (0.5 being the thinnest and 0.9 the thickest). The pencil leads are also available with different hardness and even colors, and they always stay sharp! Try the kind that come with a soft white eraser, which tends to erase better and cleaner.

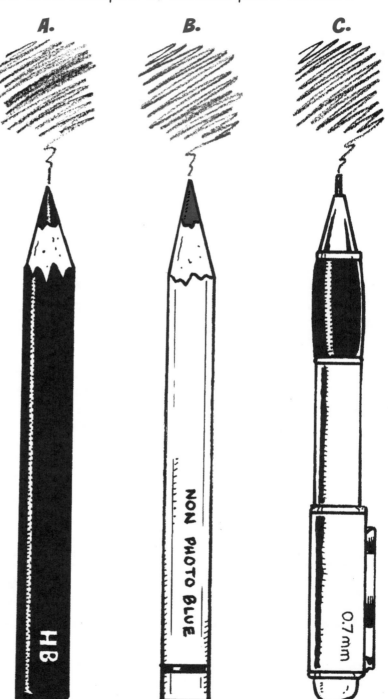

And remember, whatever type of pencil you choose, and whatever level of hardness or softness it has, try not to press to hard on your paper. Your inkers will appreciate it. Pressing to hard may cause grooves in the paper, causing ink spatters from inking tools whose tips get caught in it. Also, lighter pencil marks are easier to erase if you mess up!

It's Letter Perfect!

Lettering is also an important factor to the overall look of the graphic novel. It's used to progress the narrative, express sound effects, and show dialogue between characters. This dialogue is placed within **Word Balloons**. Some common word balloon shapes are:

THE CIRCLE AND ELLIPSE ARE THE MOST COMMON WORD BALLOON SHAPES. THEY'RE USED FOR REGULAR SPEECH.

THOUGHT BALLOONS ARE USED TO SHOW WHAT A CHARACTER IS THINKING!

THE RECTANGLE WITH ROUNDED EDGES IS ANOTHER COMMON WORD BALLON SHAPE. IT'S SOMETIMES USED FOR CHARACTERS THAT ARE A LITTLE "STIFF", LIKE ROBOTS.

STARBURST WORD BALLOONS ARE USED WHEN A CHARACTER IS YELLING!

Today, most comic book lettering is done on the computer using graphics software. However, some letterers still prefer to do lettering by hand. They believe that handlettering adds more character than the always perfect computer fonts. When it's done by hand, the letterer writes the words and word balloons **before** the drawing reaches the inker.

WRITE *NEATLY!!*

When lettering by hand, it's best to begin by drawing guidelines for the letters. This will ensure that your words are straight and your lines are even. Professional letterers use a T-square and an **Ames Lettering Guide,** a tool that, when used with the T-square, allows you to quickly draw guidelines. Circle and ellipse templates are also helpful in creating the word balloon.

Effective Lettering!

The letterer is also responsible for creating the **Sound Effects** text for the graphic novel. With SFX, the letterer can be a little more creative with the look of the fonts. Many times he/she will style the font to work better with the sound in question. For instance, if the sound is a RUMBLE, the font may have a shaky outline to resemble movement.

It's important when handlettering effects to keep the weight of the letters similar to each other within each word. For example, in the word "KA-BOOM" above, all the letters are of similar thickness and have line shading along the bottom. Similarly, the word "POW" has letters of the same thickness that seem to belong to the same font family.

KA-BOOM!

POW!

Into The Inkwell!

Contrary to popular belief, inkers do a lot more than just "trace" the penciler's artwork. It's the responsibility of the inker to reinforce the pencil lines with ink, as well as add weight and variety of line to the overall art.

You can use any black ink pen, marker, or dip pen you'd like. When it comes down to it, the tool is a matter of preference. The things to look for in an inking tool are one with a good variety of line, and an ease of control without making too much of a mess! Usually, an inker finds that more than one tool is necessary to complete the art. Here are examples of common inking tools:

Felt-tip Marker!
Pros: A felt-tip marker will give you a strong black line and they're easy to find at the art store.
Cons: Unless it's brand new, it won't give you a variety of line (thick to thin). They wear out quickly and the tip gets fat fast.

Thin Artists' Pen!
Pros: This pen gives a nice thin consistent line, great for outlining panels. The ink is waterproof India Ink, a favorite of many artists.
Cons: To get a line variety, you'll have to go over the line repeatedly.

Brush Pen!
Pros: Like the artists' pen, the ink is waterproof India Ink. It allows you to achieve a nice line variety.
Cons: After using it for a while, the tip gets soft and the lines get progressively thicker.

Brush!
Pros: A standard tool for illustration professionals. Depending on the brush quality, you can get great variety of line.
Cons: It takes a lot of practice to get good at using a brush. The really good brushes can be expensive and require separate ink.

Dip Pen!
Pros: Another standard tools for pros. Depending on the nib, you can get very different lines.
Cons: It also takes practice to get good at using it. The nib can spatter ink if it hits a groove on the paper and requires separate ink.

Into The Inkwell!

Like many artists, inkers bring their own style to the graphic novel. For instance, an inker may follow the penciler's line art exactly, or may choose to inject a personal style to the drawing.

The examples above show the same drawing inked with different styles. One style uses thinner lines with line shading, while the other utilizes thicker lines with areas of black. There's no correct style. It's just a matter of preference and technique.

Use the space below to pencil a drawing of your hero. Then use the marker provided with this book, or inking tools you've bought at an art store to ink the drawing.

Colorful Personalities!

Like lettering, today's graphic novel coloring is done mostly on a computer using the latest graphics software. There was a time, however, that coloring was done by hand using mediums, such as watercolors, colored pencils, and markers.

When using markers or colored pencils, remember that you won't be able to undo what you've done. You can erase colored pencils, but usually the complete color won't come out — especially if you pressed hard on the pencil. That's why you should color on copies of your inked work. That way, if you mess up, you always have the original to make more copies. If you're working at a size larger than your final book, reduce the art to its final size before coloring.

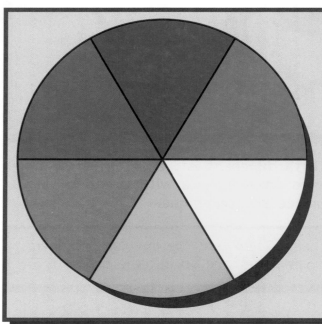

Wheelin' & Dealin'!

The **Color Wheel** shows the colors and their relationship to each other. Red, blue, and yellow are **Primary Colors**. Primary colors are colors that can't be created by mixing other colors. Between them are purple, green, and orange. These are known as **Secondary Colors**, colors that are created by mixing two primary colors. For instance, mixing red and blue makes purple, blue and yellow make green, and yellow and red make orange. The colors that "point" to each other are **Complementary Colors**, colors that go well together. Examples are red and green, blue and orange, and yellow and purple.

Colors can also define mood, temperature and atmosphere. They indicate whether something is hot and fiery, or cold and snowy. Examples of cool colors are blue and purple. Examples of warm colors are red, orange, and yellow.

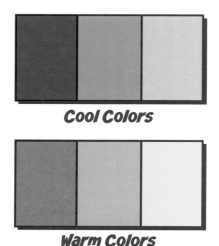

Cool Colors

Warm Colors

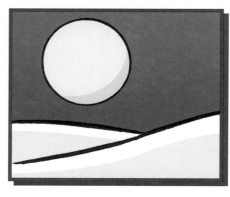

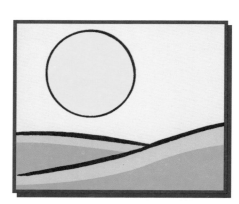

Both drawings above are the same line art. However, the use of color determines if the setting is a frozen tundra or a blazing desert!

Colorful Personalities!

It is important to work from light colors to dark colors. For example, if you want to add shadow to the yellow above, start with the yellow and then add the darker orange or brown to create the shading. Light colors over dark colors won't show.

Color the page by laying down your main colors first. In the example above, these would be the colors of his skin, hair, and outfit, as well as the color of the wall behind him. Then go back and add shadows where they're needed. Be aware of the light source in the panel before you add shadows. Also, shadows are seldom gray or black. They're usually a darker version of the base color. For instance, if the character's hair is a yellow, the shadow color would be a darker gold. With shadows come highlights. If you're coloring by hand, keep in mind where these highlights will be so you can leave some of the white paper exposed. Or you can go back after you've colored the piece with **Process White** or white paint to add highlights.

Colorful Tips!

One thing to keep in mind when coloring with markers: Depending on the quality of markers and paper you have, markers may **bleed**! In this case, bleeding means the ink from your marker may spread slightly through the weave of your paper (go to page 44 for another definition for "bleed"). This will give the appearance that you didn't color within the lines. Sometimes it affects the ink line and gives your drawing a **blurry** look. If you have think this will happen, color a bit inside the line and let the color bleed to the line. This is another reason why it's a good idea to make copies of your art before coloring the drawing!

Going Under Cover!

But wait! Before you can finish your graphic novel, you have to come up with a great cover! Something that tells the reader, "Buy this graphic novel, 'cuz there's a really great story and great art inside!" The cover should sum up what the graphic novel's all about. Is your story suspenseful? Action-packed? Romantic? Use the cover to tell that to your buyer!

For the cover image, many artists like to choose a scene from the climax of the story. Sometimes it's a drawing of an exact moment in the story. Other times it's a more **Conceptual** illustration. This means that it expresses an idea more than an actual action. For instance, a drawing of the city with the hero standing over it with his arms crossed would be a conceptual cover. Unless the hero is a really tall giant, the drawing of the hero over the city implies the idea that the hero is standing guard over the city.

Two things to consider before starting a cover:

1. What good is the cover without the title? Make sure to leave room for the title along the top and don't draw anything important that the title may cover.

2. The cover **bleeds!** This means that the art goes all the way to the edges of the paper. So draw at least ¼ inch (6 mm) past the drawing's edges.

Now you're ready to start laying out the cover by drawing a bunch of **Thumbnail Sketches!** Just like when you do your page layouts, these thumbnails are to scribble your ideas down as to how your cover will look.

This layout has the main character flying over the skyline. Pretty cool, but it could be more exciting.

The second one shows the villain looking over the hero. Interesting concept, but a little vague.

The third one has an interesting view point, and shows the hero in danger, but can still be more exciting.

This layout is action packed, and also shows the Egyptian sarcophagus, a design element vital to the story!

Going Under Cover!

Once you've settled on a cover image, create a tighter, more detailed drawing. Then, using the sketch as your guide, redraw the image from scratch on a blank sheet of bristol board. Or you can take the finished sketch and enlarge it to the working size with a copier or your computer, put the sheet of bristol board over it, and trace the final cover illustration.

And here's the final penciled cover drawing! It's action-packed, exciting and screams, **"Buy this book!"**

Once you've finished your cover, you can add the title, the issue number, and maybe a **Blurb,** or small caption, that retells what the story is about.

Use the markers provided with this book, or inking tools you've bought at an art store to ink and color the cover.

Finished Page!

The page to the right shows what a finished graphic novel page looks like penciled, inked, and colored. Below is the full script the page is based on. Study how the script and the page relate to each other. Remember, the aspect ratio of this book is 9 x 11 (22cm x 28cm), different from the final graphic novel print size of 6¾ x 10¼ (17cm x 26cm).

PAGE ONE:

PANEL ONE: Millenniapolis skyline at night. The lit windows look like stars against the silhouetted buildings.

> CAPTION: Midnight falls on the city of Millenniapolis. The streets are empty and the buildings are quiet.

PANEL TWO: Shot of the front facade of the Millenniapolis Museum of History. The building is mostly dark, with the exception of a light emanating from one of the windows.

> CAPTION: But as the city sleeps, there are those who try to take advantage of its slumber.

PANEL THREE: Inside the museum, a security guard notices a light emanating from the Ancient Egypt room.

> DIALOGUE:
> Guard: "Charlie, this is Pete. There's movement in the Egypt room. I'm gonna investigate."

PANEL FOUR: Closer shot on the guard. A silhouetted figure rises behind him.

> DIALOGUE:
> Radio: "Hold on a sec, Pete. I'm sending backup. Wait for Hector!"

PANEL FIVE: The security guard gets hit on the back of the head and falls unconscious.

> SFX: WHAK!

MIDNIGHT FALLS ON THE CITY OF *MILLENNIAPOLIS.* THE STREETS ARE EMPTY AND THE BUILDINGS ARE QUIET.

BUT AT THE *MILLENNIAPOLIS MUSEUM OF HISTORY,* THERE ARE THOSE WHO TRY TO TAKE ADVANTAGE OF ITS SLUMBER.

EXPLORE THE ICE AGE

THE SECRETS OF EGYPT
ON EXHIBIT NOW!

DISCOVER THE BRONZE AGE!

CHARLIE, THIS IS PETE. THERE'S MOVEMENT IN THE *ANCIENT EGYPT* ROOM. I'M GONNA INVESTIGATE!

HOLD ON A SEC, PETE. I'M SENDING *BACKUP.* WAIT FOR HECTOR.

TORK

WHAK!

Coloring Time!

Now it's time to get those markers out! To the right is an inked page for you to color! Remember, you can make a copy of the inked page before you color it in case you need to start over!

PAGE TWO:

PANEL ONE: Worms eye view: Close-up of the guard unconscious in the foreground. His assailant is walking away from him into the Egypt room.

DIALOGUE:
Radio: "Pete, do you hear me? Pete!"

PANEL TWO: The large figure steps into the light. He's a large, muscular man dressed in the costume of an Egyption guard. He walks towards a smaller older man whose costume has hints of Ancient Egypt. He is **Dr. Ankh.**

DIALOGUE:
Pasheri: "We gotta go, Dr. Ankh!"

Dr. Ankh: "Beautiful, isn't it, **Pasheri?**

PANEL THREE: Close-up of Dr. Ankh's face.

DIALOGUE:
Dr. Ankh: "I've searched for it for decades!"

PANEL FOUR: Reverse shot revealing the museum room. A large sarcophagus sits against a wall.

DIALOGUE:
Dr. Ankh: " Within this sarcophagus lies a jewel of great power called the **Eye of Wepwawet.** With it I will be able to rule the world!"

Voice from off panel: "You'll have to get past me first, Ankh!"

PETE, DO YOU *HEAR* ME?! PETE!!

WE GOTTA GO, *DR. ANKH!*

BEAUTIFUL, ISN'T IT, PASHERI?

I'VE SEARCHED FOR IT FOR *DECADES!*

WITHIN THIS SARCOPHAGUS LIES A *JEWEL* OF GREAT POWER CALLED *THE EYE OF WEPWAWET!*

WITH IT I WILL BE ABLE TO *RULE THE WORLD!*

YOU'LL HAVE TO GET PAST ME FIRST, ANKH!

It's your turn to be the inker! Ink the penciled blueline drawing on the next page, which is based on this script! Use the markers that are packaged with this book or inking tools you've bought at an art store!

PAGE THREE:

PANEL ONE: **Millennium Man** hovers in a heroic pose over Dr. Ankh.

> DIALOGUE:
> Dr. Ankh: "Millennium Man! Impressive! You've arrived earlier than I calculated you would."

PANEL TWO: Dr. Ankh points his hand at Millennium Man. His hand glows bright and fires a beam.

> DIALOGUE:
> Dr. Ankh: "I will not underestimate you again!"

> SFX: ZZRAK!!

PANEL THREE: Millennium Man gets struck by the beam.

> DIALOGUE:
> Millennium Man: "AARGH!!"

> SFX: Z-KOW!!

Break Out Your Pencils!

Sharpen those pencils! Keep those erasers handy! It's time for you to be the penciler! To the right are breakdowns, which means the blocking out of the layout and character placement. Add the details to the breakdowns and finish the page!

PAGE FOUR:

PANEL ONE: Worms-Eye View of a smoldering Millennium Man lying groggily on the floor. Pasheri stands over him menacingly.

> DIALOGUE:
> Pasheri: "**This** is the great Millennium Man?"

PANEL TWO: Pasheri raises his arm back to hit Millennium Man.

> DIALOGUE:
> Pasheri: "I'm not impressed."

PANEL THREE: Close-up of Millennium Man's face looking up towards Pasheri.

> DIALOGUE:
> Millennium Man: "!"

PANEL FOUR:Close-up of Millennium Man catching Pasheri's fist.

> SFX: FAP!

PANEL FIVE: Large panel of Millennium Man punching Pasheri.

> DIALOGUE:
> Millennium Man: "Impressed now?"

> SFX: POW!!

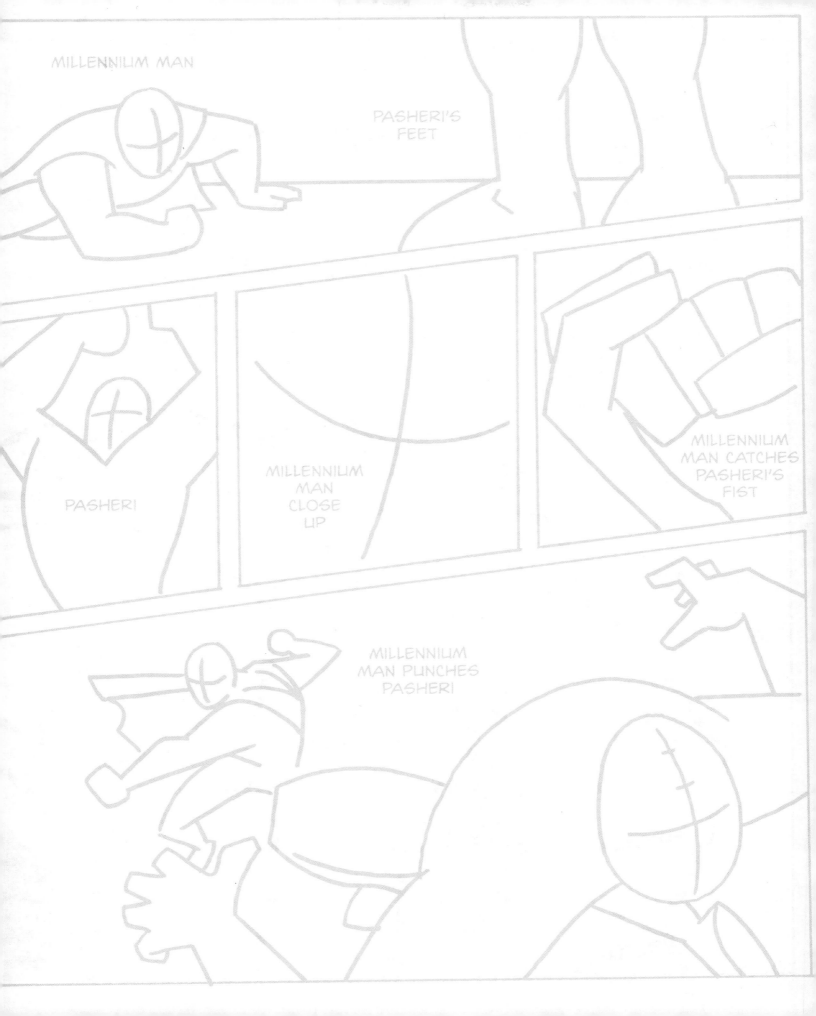

Glossary of Terms!

Ames Lettering Guide: A small, plastic device used to draw guidelines for lettering

Bird's Eye View: A view from above the action; gives the reader a detached feeling and lets them see the action from an unusual perspective

Bleed: When the ink from the marker spreads through the weave of the paper; In page layout, when the ink prints to the edge of the paper

Blueline: Drawing created or printed with a light blue ink or pencil that doesn't reproduce when copied

Breakdowns: The blocking out of the layout and character placement

Bristol Board: The drawing paper usually used by illustrators to draw graphic novels

Caption: Text used as narrative to progress the story

Cast Shadow: The darkest area created by a light source; shadow created by an object on another object

Closeup: A tight shot of a characters face or an object; if it's a person, it's devised to show emotion; if it's an object, then it highlights the importance of that object

Color Wheel: Diagram that shows the colors and their relationship to each other

Colorist: Artist who applies color to the inked artwork

Complementary Colors: Colors opposite each other on the color wheel; examples are red and green, blue and orange, and yellow and purple.

Crosshatching: Overlapping diagonal pencil or ink strokes used for shading

Crow Quill Pen: Sharp pointed pen dipped in ink and used for inking

Establishing Shot: A shot which sets the location of where the action is taking place; many times it's the first panel of the page where the beginning of the scene takes place

Extreme Closeup: Similar to a closeup, but even closer (i.e., a person's eyes)

Glossary of Terms!

Foreshortening: The figure drawn in perspective as if the figure or object is coming right out at the viewer

French Curve: A plastic device used to draw curves and ellipses

Gutter: The space between the panels

Highlights: The area on an object that's the brightest, being closest to the light source

Horizon Line: In drawing perspective, the eye level of the viewer in relation to the scene

Inker: Artist who reinforces the pencil drawing by using ink and a variety of pens

Layout: Arrangement of the panels and artwork on the page

Lightboard: Lit drawing board used to see through layers of paper

Light Source: The direction from which the light comes from

Line of Action: Imaginary line running through the figure that determines the body's curve

Long Shot: A shot that establishes a connection between two characters or between a character and a thing; it's best used for dialogue and usually shows the full characters from head to toe

Medium Shot: Similar to a "long shot," but shows the characters from the waist up

One-Point Perspective: Perspective with one vanishing point

P.O.V.: Point of view

Pacing: The speed of the story

Panel: A frame in which a moment of a story's action is drawn

Penciler: Artist who draws the bulk of the art in a graphic novel; the penciler is responsible for translating the script into panels of drawings

Glossary of Terms!

Perspective: The appearance of depth and distance on a two-dimensional surface

Plot: The overall storyline of the graphic novel

Primary Colors: Colors that can't be created by mixing other colors: red, blue, and yellow

Script: The detailed storyline, including dialogue and other art descriptions

Splash Page: A panel of art that takes up a whole page in a graphic novel; usually consists of an action or scene extremely exciting or important to the story

Stippling: Dot pattern used for shading and created by tapping the inking tool repeatedly on the paper

T-square: A straight-edge with a perpendicular piece at one end

Texture: The surface characteristic of an object

Thought Balloon: Shape consisting of the words a character is thinking

Thumbnail: Small rough sketches created to work out a larger drawing

Two-Point Perspective: Perspective with two vanishing points

Wide Shot: See Establishing Shot

Word Balloon: Shape consisting of the dialogue a character is speaking

Worm's Eye View: A view from under the action looking up; lets the reader feel that they're in the middle of the action

Vanishing Point: The point where all parallel perspective lines appear to come together

Just The FAQs!

How do I break into comics?

As an illustrator you have to build a strong portfolio! Include a few samples of 4-5 page stories, not just pin-ups of a character in a heroic pose. If your goal is to be a penciler, have pencil samples. If you want to be an inker, have inked samples, preferably over someone else's pencils. If you want to be either, have both penciled and inked samples, but separate.

It's also a very good idea to start attending **Comic Book Conventions.** That's a great opportunity to meet industry professionals and get feedback of your work. Remember, when professionals critique your work, make sure you keep an open mind and a thick skin. They'll give you honest opinions which may seem harsh to the sensitive artist, but they're only trying to be helpful.

Contact or visit the website of the company you want to submit to for their specific submission guidelines. Many times their websites also have sample scripts that you can draw and submit. And remember to *practice, practice, practice!*

What is a Copyright?

A copyright is a legal document granting creators ownership of their creation. It's represented by the "©" symbol followed by the date. This means that one creator cannot publish a graphic novel using another creator's work without permission.

What is Self-Publishing?

Self-publishing is when a creator publishes the graphic novel, as opposed to one of the large publishing company. The creator gets all the profits, but also has to pay for everything.

How do I get my graphic novel into comic book stores?

Some store owners will allow creators to sell their graphic novels at their stores for a small percentage of the profits.

How can I promote my graphic novel?

One of the easiest and least-expensive ways to promote your graphic novel is to create a website promoting your characters and stories. There are many online companies that offer free hosting where you can build simple websites. Include a couple of pages from your graphic novels!